ARTISAN BREAD

COOKBOOK

FOR BEGINNERS

Easy, Quick and Delicious Recipes for Perfect Homemade Bread

TRACY GORDON

TABLE OF CONTENT

Chapter 1:

INTRODUCTION

Artisan Bread

Artisan Bread is highly wanted by individuals searching for a rich, regular tasting natural loaf that is expertly hand created with care. The ingredients that are found in a typical Artisan Bread recipe are water, yeast, salt, and flour. There are times when milk or oil is added to the essential ingredients to deliver particular varieties of bread. Different recipes use cheese, fruit, nuts and other delicious ingredients to make a particular flavor. This richness of flavor is the key in any traditional Artisan bread, which tremendously differs from the mass-created vacuum package varieties found in your nearby market. Although they don't have time because of the absence of preservatives and chemicals. Artisan Bread gives a healthier, more delicious, and welcome alternative to the usual bland loaves customers normally buy.

There are a wide variety of Artisan breads accessible - each with its different formula. For instance, French Baguettes, Italian Focaccia, Deli-style Rye Bread, and some more. To make a successful version of one of these Artisan Breads, cautious consideration must be paid to the preparation and baking process. Traditional bakers depend on hand kneading the dough as opposed to using electric blenders to control the degree of gluten strands. The division and shaping of dough are likewise significant since specific varieties must be created and shaped through folding, braiding, and different methods. The baking procedure is normally done in stone or block hearths with natural heat, using baking stones to circulate heat and produce a pleasant, even crust. Artisan Bread Recipes have been made for pizza coverings, loaves for submarine sandwiches and hoagies, decadent croissants, and stuffed loaves filled up with delicious fillers. A prime cause of a brilliant Artisan stuffed loaf is from a desert variety - the chocolate-infused loaf. This Artisan Bread features chocolate chips and cocoa in the dough and used as filler when the loaf is framed.

This flavorful bread can undoubtedly be made at home, without looking for nearby Artisan pastry kitchens. A kitchen with the correct ingredients and tools will suffice. The most ideal approach to start this is, to begin with, the basic recipe (flour, salt, water, and yeast) and acquaint new ingredients to alter the flavor as proficiency increases. Fancier loaves use honey, or oil to add to the moisture content of the bread. Firmer dough can be accomplished by permitting the dough to settle to extra time before kneading and folding.

Start by blending the ingredients well, until there is a firm structure that is similarly mixed. Knead and fold the dough until it arrives at a predictable texture throughout. Place this dough in an oiled bowl and cover it - allow the dough to rise (as the yeast is enacted) until it has multiplied in size. At the point when the dough has arrived at an acceptable size, divide the mass of dough into separate lumps and structure these shapes to fit into available pans. A substitute strategy is to shape a huge lump and place it in the center point of a baking stone. Preheat the oven for baking, and ensure it is prepared once the dough has been divided and formed. Place the dough into the oven, and cautiously keep tabs on it to guarantee that the dough is thoroughly baked. Alterations should be made to build up the loaf to its maximum capacity. when the dough has completed the process of baking, remove it from the oven and allow it to cool before serving. The leftover warmth keeps on baking the loaf slightly, so don't be too anxious to even think about cutting it open and release all the steam inside if the crumb (delicate inside of the bread) will be softened.

A BASIC GUIDE TO DIFFERENT TYPES OF ARTISANAL BREAD

Genuine handmade breads have four fundamental ingredients in them – wheat flour, yeast, salt, and water. Sometimes, sourdough might be used rather than yeast as a raising operator. Flavorings, for example, flavors, herbs, nuts, fruit, and cheese may likewise be added for variety. What sets an Artisan bread apart from common bread are the strategies used in making it.

ARTISAN BREADS – DIFFERENT TYPES

COUNTRY LOAF

This round and dried up bread is ideal for making a liberal Bruschetta. Just toast it and enjoy with any of your preferred ingredients. It has an unmistakable porous surface which makes it perfect for serving with supper or lunch. It supplements food with sauces, dried meats, and cheeses.

BAGUETTE

This French bread is famous. These thin, long loaves of bread have been made for a considerable length of time in France. Some type of steam is required in the stove while preparing this bread as it permits the crust of the brad to extend before setting, which makes a lot lighter loaf. It additionally lends the outside of the bread a glazed appearance. Baguettes are best consumed within of preparing.

SOURDOUGH

This is particular, heavy bread that can be temperamental and requesting; no yeast is used to make this bread and lactobacillus culture is used as a starter. When contrasted with yeast-based bread, sourdough has an exceptionally particularly, sour and tangy taste, basically as a result of the lactic acid that the lactobacilli created.

CIABATTA

The strict meaning of the word Ciabatta is slippering and the bread gets its name from its shape. This is an Italian white bread that is commonly used to make sandwiches. It's humble-looking, soggy yet airy, delicious yet crusty, and ideal for even the most discerning palates.

MEDITERRANEAN BREAD

This bread is ordinarily made with French flour. Sundried tomatoes, red and green, dried peppers are used in ideal union with different herbs to make this impeccably delicious, genuinely Mediterranean style bread.

WALNUT COB

This exceptionally particular bread is made using a blend of dark rye flour, French flour, and malted flour; every one of these ingredients is used in the correct extent to make a malty-flavored bread that is full of walnuts. If you are searching for a gourmet bread to add to a supper or lunch spread, this is the one.

RYE BREAD

This bread is produced using rye grain flour and wheat flour. The color of the rye chooses how thick or dark the bread will be. Rye bread is high in fiber contrasted with most other standard breads and has an extremely solid flavor as well.

WALNUT & RAISIN BREAD

This is extraordinary bread that is a mix of sesame seeds, poppy seeds, wholemeal flour, oats and pumpkin seeds, raisins, and walnuts. It's incredibly nutritious and has an unmistakable flavor as well. It helps catch and dispose of fats in the stomach related procedure. It goes very well with soups and cheeses and saves well for a few days.

PAIN BRIOCHE

It is viewed as a Viennoiserie and accepted to have Norman origins. While it's made like most different breads, it is richer in texture a lot of like a pastry as it contains milk, eggs and in some cases some sugar as well. Pain Brioche can be eaten with jam and nectar and used to make French toast as well.

Chapter 2:

COUNTY LOAF RECIPE

INGREDIENTS

FOR THE STARTER AND LEAVEN

- 1000 grams white-bread flour

- 1000 grams entire wheat flour

- FOR THE BREAD

- 200 grams leaven

- 900 grams white-bread flour

- 100 grams entire wheat flour, also more for dusting

- 20 grams fine sea salt

- 100 grams rice flour

PREPARATION

- Make the starter: Mix 1,000 grams white-bread flour with 1,000 grams entire wheat flour. Put 100 grams of warm water (around 80 degrees) in a little container or holder and include 100 grams of the flour blend. Utilize your fingers to blend until altogether consolidated and the blend is the consistency of thick batter. Spread with a towel and let sit at room temperature until blend starts to air bubble and puff, 2 to 3 days.

- At the point when the starter starts to give signs of action, start regular feedings. Keep the starter at room temperature, and simultaneously every day discard of 80 percent of the starter and feed the remaining starter with a balance of warm water and white-wheat flour blend (50 grams of each is fine). At the point when starter starts to rise and fall typically and takes on a somewhat sour smell, it's prepared; this should take around 1 week. (Reserve remaining flour blend for leaven.)

- Make the leaven: The prior night baking, discard everything except 1 tablespoon of the mature starter. Blend the rest of the starter in with 200 grams of warm water and mix with your hand to scatter. Include 200 grams of the white-wheat flour blend and consolidate well. Spread with a towel and let rest at room temperature for 12 hours or until circulated air through and puffed in appearance. To test readiness, drop a tablespoon of leaven into a bowl of room-temperature water; if that it floats it's prepared to utilize. If it doesn't, permit more time to ferment.

- Make the dough: In a big bowl, mix 200 grams of leaven with 700 grams of warm water and mix to scatter. (Save remaining leaven for future loaves)

- Include 900 grams of white-bread flour and 100 grams of entire wheat flour to bowl and utilize your hands to blend until no traces of dry flour remain. The dough will be sticky and ragged. Close up bowl with a towel and let mixture rest for 25 to 40 minutes at room temperature.

- Include 20 grams fine sea salt and 50 grams of warm water. Use hands to coordinate salt and water into dough completely. The dough will start to pull apart, yet keep blending; it will return together.

- Cover up the dough with a towel and move to a warm area, 75 to 80 degrees ideally (like close to a window in a bright room, or inside a turned-off stove). Allow dough rise for 30 minutes. Crease dough by plunging a hand in the water, grabbing hold of the underside of the dough at one quadrant, and extending it up over the remainder of the dough. Repeat this activity 3 additional occasions, rotating bowl a quarter turn for each overlay. Do this each half-hour for 2 1/2 hours progressively (3 hours complete). The dough ought to be rolling and increment in volume 20 to 30 percent. If not, keep on letting rise and fold for as long as an hour more.

- Move dough to a work surface and residue top with flour. Utilize a mixture scrubber to cut dough into 2 equivalent pieces and flip them over so floured sides are face down. Crease the cut side of each piece up onto itself so the flour on a surface remains altogether outwardly of the loaf; this will end up being the outside layer. Work dough into rigid rounds. Spot the dough rounds on a work surface, spread with a towel, and let rest 30 minutes.

- Blend 100 grams entire wheat flour and 100 grams rice flours. Line two 10-to 12-inch bread-sealing baskets or blending bowls in with towels. Utilize a portion of the flour blend to generously flour towels (hold remaining blend).

- Dust rounds with entire wheat flour. Utilize a dough scrubber to flip them over onto a work surface so floured sides are looking down. Take one round, and begin along the edge nearest to you, pull the last 2 corners of the mixture down toward you, at that point fold them up into the center third of the dough. Repeat this activity on the privilege and left sides, pulling the edges out and folding them in over the inside. At long last, lift the top corners and fold down over past folds. (Envision folding a bit of paper in on itself from each of the 4 sides.) Roll mixture over so the folded side turns into the base of the loaf. Shape into a smooth, rigid ball. Repeat with other rounds.

- Transfer rounds, crease side up, to arranged crates. Spread with a towel and return mixture to the 75-to 80-degree condition for 3 to 4 hours. (Or then again let dough rise for 10 to 12 hours in the refrigerator. Take back to room temperature before baking.)

- Around 30 minutes before preparing, place a Dutch oven or lidded cast-iron pot in the stove and warm it to 500 degrees. Dust the tops of the dough, still in their containers, with whole wheat/rice-flour mixture. Carefully remove warmed pot from stove and delicately turn 1 portion into pan crease side down. Utilize a lame (a baker's blade) or extremely sharp steel to score the top of the bread a couple of times to consider development, cover and move to the stove. Decrease temperature to 450 degrees and cook for 20 minutes. Cautiously remove cover (steam may discharge) and cook for 20 additional minutes or until the crust layer is a rich, brilliant brown color.

- Move bread to a wire rack to cool for 15 minutes before cutting. The base of the loaf should sound empty when tapped. Increase stove temperature to 500 degrees, clear out a pot and repeat this procedure with the second loaf.

Chapter 3:

THE BAGUETTE RECIPE

When you picture a scene in France, do you imagine a young lady in a striped top, wearing a beret, and riding a bike with a bushel loaded with long portions of French bread? Those long loaves are called "baguettes." (The term originates from the Latin word for "stick.") They are iconic, and France's notoriety for incredibly crusty up and tasty loaves is known far and wide.

They state that nothing can come close to the bread you can get in France. I've never been, so I can't state without a doubt, however, I think you'd have the most ideal potential for success if you make it yourself. That is to say, how might anything be superior to a newly baked portion of bread? That crackly crust, the delicate, airy crumb inside, hot and yeasty and simply asking to be attacked!

Check out it. It'll just take 4 basic fixings and a couple of simple advances. It's for the most part downtime!

Ingredients

- 75 ounces warm water
- 1 1/2 teaspoons dynamic dry yeast

- 16 ounces bread flour

- 2 teaspoons genuine salt

- 10 ounces cool water (you may not require the entirety of the water)

- additional flour, for dusting

Fast Instructions

1. Measure the warm water in a little bowl and sprinkle the yeast on top. Put in a safe spot.

2. Measure the bread flour into a huge bowl and mix in the salt.

3. Make a well in the focal point of the flour blend, and mix in the dissolved yeast.

4. Add the cool water, a little at once, while blending, just until a shaggy dough has framed (you should not utilize the entirety of the water).

5. Cover the bowl and permit it to rest for 30 minutes.

6. Transfer the dough to a floured work surface, and tenderly press it into a square shape and crease into thirds. Turn 90 degrees and repeat this.

7. Place the dough in a huge oiled bowl, and spread with cling wrap. Permit it to rise in a warm spot for 1 to 2 hours, or until multiplied in mass.

8. Divide the batter into 4 equivalent parts, and shape every one into a long portion (around 15-inches in length and 1/2-creeps in width), with pointed closures.

9. Place the portions on a floured towel, spread with oiled saran wrap, and permit to ascend for 30 to 45 minutes.

10. Preheat the broiler to 450 degrees F, and place a skillet of water on the base rack.

11. Uncover the baguettes and move to gently greased baking sheets.

12. Sprinkle with flour, and make 4 extended cuts down everyone with a lame, razor, or a sharp blade.

13. Bake the breads for 35 to 40 minutes, or until hard and brown. (The baguettes should give an empty sound when tapped.)

Step by step instructions to make a crusty French BAGUETTE

1. Start by dissolving the yeast in warm water.

2. While that is doing its magic, mix the flour and salt. Make somewhat well in the middle, and include the yeast. Mix it around, taking flour from the outside edge and carrying it into the well, a little at once.

3. Next, include a touch of cool water. Continue blending, and including water varying, until a shaggy batter structures. Presently simply spread it freely, and let it rest.

4. For this sort of bread, there's not a great deal of kneading included. It just needs a couple of fast folds, to get smooth and manufacture quality, without working the gluten and causing sturdiness.

5. Place the dough into a greased container and cover it firmly. Permit it to proof (or rise) in a warm spot until multiplied in mass.

6. Divide the mixture into 4 equivalent parts, and shape into long logs (around 15 inches in length) with pointed ends. Settle the portions into a floured kitchen towel, spread with oiled cling wrap, and permit to rise a second time.

7. While the loaves are rising, fill a heating dish with water and place it in the base of your oven. Preheat the broiler

and permit it to load up with steam from the water. This is the KEY to a crusty up roll.

8. Once the loaves have completed their second rise, remove the saran wrap and sprinkle them with a little flour. At that point rapidly cut them with a lame, extremely sharp blaze, or sharp knife. This is beautiful, yet it likewise permits the crust to break and the bread to extend in a more controlled way.

9. Place them in the stove and let them prepare until deep brilliant brown. They should feel light and dry outside, and when you tap them they should give an empty sound.

AUTHENTIC FRENCH BAGUETTE RECIPE

How To Use A Baguette

This type of loaf is infinitely versatile!

Cut it into 1/2-inch rounds and its ideal as a base for bruschetta or crostini. Or on the other hand, it tends to be utilized as a scoop for your preferred party dip. What's more, we love it toasted with garlic spread, for garlic bread. So great with a pasta supper!

Or then again simply tear it and eat it with a hot bowl of soup.

So fulfilling!

STEPS TO KEEP A FRENCH BREAD BAGUETTE FRESH

Baguettes are best when they're newly prepared, yet they're still lovely darn incredible following a couple of days!

To store a French roll, simply wrap it freely and save it at room temperature for 2 or more days. If you notice it's not as dried up sooner or later, simply pop it in a warm oven(around 170 degrees) for 5 or 10 minutes, and it will come out great.

Would you be able to FREEZE A BAGUETTE?

An extravagant French Boulanger probably won't agree with me on this one, however, I state put it all on the line!

I do this a great deal at my home. At the point when the loaf is still new, cut it down into thin rounds. I'll regularly cut on the corner to corner so there is increased surface area to spread yummy things on. At that point simply slip the roll cuts into a zip-top cooler pack, and into the cooler, they all go. Whenever we need a cut of hard French bread, we simply pull out what we need.

The roll cuts defrost in only a few minutes at room temp. Or then again they can be warmed in the oven or toasted up. It's too advantageous!

Chapter 4:

THE SOURDOUGH RECIPE

Before you start, you'll need a sourdough starter.

On the off chance that you don't have a starter, you can make your own or buy one.

A sourdough starter is a live culture produced using flour and water. When combined, the blend will begin to ferment which builds up the normally happening wild yeasts and bacteria present inside the blend. A little part of this culture is utilized to make your bread rise.

It doesn't stop there.

Your starter should be kept alive with standard feedings of flour and water to keep up its quality for the most extreme rising force. It's all a piece of the procedure, like taking care of a pet.

The most effective method to FEED YOUR STARTER

Each baker has their strategy, and with training, you'll, in the end, build up your everyday routine

To start, pour off a portion of the culture (about half) and afterward feed it with equivalent loads of flour and water. Whisk well with a fork until it's without lump. Let it rest at room temperature or in a warm spot until it turns out to be bubbly and doubles in size. At that point, you can utilize it to make bread dough. This can take somewhere in the range of 2-12 hours or all the more relying upon temperature and the state of your starter. Show restraint!

Float Test: If you're as yet uncertain whether your starter is prepared, drop a modest quantity (around 1 tsp) into a glass of water; on the off chance that it floats to the top it very well may be utilized. On the off chance that it sinks, your starter ought to be taken care of once more.

WHERE TO OBTAIN A STARTER

All sourdough starters are extraordinary. They can be produced using scratch, bought on the internet, or in case you're fortunate, somebody will share a part of their starter to you. Starters extend from thick to thin in surface and can be made with an assortment of flours. I utilize two distinct starters; one is homemade and the other was a blessing from my companion.

How to use your starter

After you have taken care of your starter, and it's bubbly and dynamic, spill some out of the container to gauge or measure. That is it. At that point, remember to take care of what's left in the container with more flour and water to prop the procedure up.

Storage Options

On the off chance that you just bake a couple of times each month, keep your starter in the fridge and feed it once per week. In case you're an eager baker, store your starter it room temperature and feed it once every day.

NOVICE SOURDOUGH BREAD RECIPE

STEP #1: MIX THE DOUGH

When your starter is active and bubbly, you can blend the mixture.

To start, whisk the starter and water together in a big bowl. This recipe likewise includes olive oil, which you'll combine with the wet ingredients. At that point, including the salt and flour. Squish the blend together with your hands until the flour is completely retained. The dough will look rough and shaggy.

Tip: for best results, gauge the entirety of your ingredients with a digital kitchen scale. You'll get more reliable outcomes as opposed to utilizing estimating cups. Additionally, use bread flour rather than generally useful flour for better gluten improvement and a higher rise.

STEP #2: AUTOLYSE

The next stage is to allow the dough to rest or 'autolyze' for around 30 minutes. This will make the mixture a lot simpler to deal with and shape.

AUTOLYSE DEFINED

This is the first resting period after you blend the mixture. It kicks off gluten improvement without kneading. Solid gluten = great bread.

For timing, autolyze can run somewhere in the range of 15 minutes to 1 hour or more, contingent upon the kind of bread you are making and your very own baking plan. I find that at least 30 minutes works best for this recipe.

*A Note on Salt-as you keep on baking you'll see that a few bakers want to include the salt simply after autolyze. This is because salt hinders the gluten development. I've followed this system for a considerable length of time, however no longer keep on doing as such, and have refreshed this section to reflect my present technique. I like to blend all of the ingredients simultaneously. It produces great loaves (besides, you won't forget to include the saltwater!). I'll leave the decision over to you.

STEP #3: LET IT RISE (BULK FERMENTATION)

When the dough has rested (autolyze), work the mixture into a ball-it doesn't need to be great.

Presently it's prepared to rise.

Now, spread your bowl with wraps and a perfect kitchen towel. Leave it in a warm, bright spot to rise. This underlying rise is additionally called the 'bulk fermentation' and is imperative to the development and quality of the dough.

Your dough is prepared when it no longer looks thick and has expanded in volume around 1/2-2x its unique size.

To what extent WILL IT TAKE?

This can take somewhere in the range of 3-12 hours relying upon the temperature of your ingredients, the intensity of your starter, and general condition. Keep in mind, since sourdough bread doesn't contain commercial yeast, it will take extensively longer to rise. In the late spring, it can take anyplace between 3-4 hours at 85 F while in the winter, around 6-12 hours at 65 F. It is critical to watch your dough and not the clock. It's prepared when it's prepared. Be flexible.

Tip: permit the dough to rise in a bowl or clear container with estimating marks. You can outwardly follow its development and won't be enticed to rush the process. On the off chance that you are as yet battling with the rise of your dough, particularly when the climate is cold (and it's taking forever!) you should seriously consider utilizing a sealing box. This is fundamentally a temperature-controlled 'greenhouse' for your dough. This is the one I use and it FOLDS FLAT.

Reward Tip: during bulk fermentation, you have the choice to play out a series of 'stretch and folds' to reinforce the dough. Just accumulate a bit of the dough, stretch it upwards, and afterward fold it over itself. Pivot the bowl 1/4 turn and repeat this procedure until you have completed the circle. For this mixture, which is very dry and not unreasonably simple to extend, repeat this method 1 to multiple times, separated 30 minutes to 1 hour apart. You don't need to be precise with your planning here don't as well, stress. Although this step isn't compulsory, it will build the all-out volume of your bread which is extremely nice.

STEP #4: CUT + SHAPE THE DOUGH

Before you start, divide your work surface down the middle; gently flour one side (for cutting) and leave the other half perfect (for molding).

Expel the mixture from the bowl, and place it onto the floured section so it doesn't stick.

Cut the mixture down the middle to make 2 loaves, or leave it whole for a single loaf.

STEP #5: CHOOSE A BAKING VESSEL

Bake sourdough in a Dutch oven.

The pot traps in warmth and moisture which is basic to preparing great bread. These components play a key job in how the slices will open up or 'bloom' and the Dutch oven assists with controlling this procedure. In this way, except if you have an expert deck stove with steam injectors, this happens to be a truly dependable other option. Go Dutch.

I've given baking pizza stones and treat plate with no karma. My bread would tear at the base and sides. I utilized different steaming techniques to cure this; anyway, I saw them as unwieldy and not reasonable for regular use. Nothing worked. The absence of moisture in my oven immediately solidified the outside of the bread before it got an opportunity to completely rise. Subsequently, it made my bread 'blow out.' Using a Dutch oven is an incredible arrangement.

STEP #6: LET IT RISE AGAIN (SECOND RISE)

After molding the dough, liberally cover the bottom of your Dutch oven with cornmeal (or line the base with non-stick material paper). On the other hand, skip the Dutch oven and utilize a sealing container.

Place the mixture inside where it should rise once more (it would be ideal if you read tip underneath it's significant).

This time, the dough will ascend for a shorter period, around 30 minutes 60 minutes. It is prepared when the dough is somewhat puffy and not, at this point thick. Once more, factors, for example, the temperature of your dough and general condition will impact the growth rate.

Tip: this specific dough is viewed as 'low hydration' which implies it doesn't contain a great deal of water. They are anything but difficult to deal with and hold their shape well indeed. That is the reason I do the second rise directly in the Dutch stove; it doesn't spread out.

Nonetheless, if you are working with a high hydration dough or if you add more water to this formula, it may spread out like a pancake because of the expanded moisture content. This is ordinary. As another option, rather than doing a free structure second rise (as demonstrated above), place the dough in a cloth-lined sealing basket or bowl. I utilize a little pyrex blending bowl. Either choice will contain the dough and hold its shape appropriately.

Oven Spring: accomplishing a good rise requires effort. *note below.

Slicing: directly before your bread goes into the stove, make a cut around 2-3 inches in length in the center point of the mixture; this permits the steam to get away and the dough to grow. You can utilize a serrated blade, paring knife, or bread lame.

- It is significant not released the second rise for a long time. This can be hard to pass judgment. 30 minutes-1 hour ought to be adequate however you should analyze and make adjustments if vital. An over-sealed dough will have depleted its strength, and your bread won't get the boost it needs to deliver a pleasant, round loaf.

STEP #7: BAKE THE SOURDOUGH BREAD

Preheat your oven to 450 F. Place your bread into the stove (top on) and lessen the temperature to 400 F. Heat for 20 minutes. At the point when you expel the cover, your bread will be pale and sparkly. Keep on preparing (revealed) for an extra 40 minutes or until deep, brilliant brown. Remember that all oven is extraordinary; you may need to make negligible changes following these temperatures.

Tip: during the most recent 10 minutes of heating, air out the oven door. This permits the moisture to escape, leaving your bread with a fresh outside. Or on the other hand, remove the bread from the pot and let it bake directly on the rack. The last delivers an increasingly fresh crust.

when the bread is prepared, remove it from the oven and move to a wire rack. Cool for in any event an hour before cutting. Try not to cut too early or probably within will have a sticky surface! Persistence.

Chapter 5:

CIABATTA RECIPE

Delicate, chewy custom made bread can't be beat!

INGREDIENTS:

FOR THE SPONGE:

- ⅛ teaspoon instant (rapid-rise yeast)

- ½ cup water (at room temperature)

- 1 cupall-flour

FOR THE DOUGH:

- ¾ cup water (at room temperature)

- ¼ cup whole or 2% milk (at room temperature)

- 2 cup sall- flour

- 1½ teaspoons salt

- ½ teaspoon instant (rapid-rise yeast)

DIRECTIONS:

1. Make the Sponge: Add the flour, water, and yeast in a

medium bowl and mix with a wooden spoon until a uniform mass forms. Spread the bowl firmly with plastic wrap and let remain at room temperature for at any rate 8 hours or as long as 24 hours.

2. Make the Dough: Place the sponge and the dough ingredients (flour, salt, yeast, water, and milk) in the bowl of a stand blender fitted with the paddle attachment. Blend on low speed until consolidated and a shaggy dough structures, around 1 moment, scratching down the bowl and paddle as needed. Speed up to medium-low and keep blending until the dough turns into a uniform mass that gathers on the paddle and pulls from the sides of the bowl, 4 to 6 minutes. Change to the dough hook and knead the bread on medium speed until smooth and gleaming (the dough will be sticky), around 10 minutes. Move the dough to a huge bowl, spread firmly with plastic wrap, and let rise at room temperature until multiplied in size, around 60 minutes.

3. Splash a rubber spatula or bowl scrubber with non-stick cooking spray. Fold the dough over itself by tenderly lifting and folding the edge of the dough toward the middle. Turn the bowl 90 degrees, and fold once more. Turn the bowl and fold the dough 6 additional occasions

(for a total of 8 times). Spread with plastic wrap and let rise for 30 minutes.

4. Repeat the folding as in step #3, replace the plastic wrap, and let rise until twice in size, around 30 minutes.

5. One hour prior baking, modify a stove rack to the lower-center position, place a baking stone on the rack and preheat the broiler to 450 degrees F.

6. Cut two 12x6-inch bits of material paper and dust generously with flour. Move the dough to a floured work surface, being mindful so as not to flatten it. Generously flour the highest point of the dough and divide it into equal parts with a bench scraper. Turn 1 bit of batter cut-side-up and dust with flour. With very much floured hands, press the dough into an unpleasant 12x6-inch square shape. Fold the shorter sides of the dough toward center, covering them like you would fold a letter in thirds, to frame a 7x4-inch square shape. Repeat with the second bit of dough.

7. Gently transfer each loaf, seam-side-down, to the material sheets, dust with flour, and spread with plastic wrap. Let the loaves sit at room temperature for 30 minutes (the outside of the loaves will grow little air

bubbles).

8. Slide the material pieces with the loaves onto a pizza peel. Utilizing floured fingertips, equitably jab the whole surface of each portion to frame a 10x6-inch square shape; spray the loaves lightly with water. Slides the loaves and material onto the baking stone. Bake, spraying the loaves with water twice more during the initial 5 minutes of baking time, until the crust is deep brilliant brown color and the loaves register 210 degrees F, 22 to 27 minutes.

9. Move the loaves to a wire rack, dispose of the material, and let cool to room temperature for at any rate 1 hour before slicing and serving. The bread can be wrapped by a twofold layer of plastic wrap and put away at room temperature for as long as 3 days. Wrapped with an extra layer of foil, the bread can be frozen for as long as 1 month. To crisp the crust, defrost the bread at room temperature (whenever solidified), and place opened up bread in a 450-degree oven for 6 to 8 minutes.

Chapter 6:

MEDITERRANEAN HOMEMADE OLIVE BREAD RECIPE

This is such a basic olive bread recipe with just five primary ingredients. Realize how easy it very well may be to simply purchase bread from the store. On the off chance that you need great bread though it merits making your own! There's so much fulfillment when you nurture something from flour, water, and yeast to a loaf of bread with a crackling crust and a smell that you'll never need to leave your kitchen.

There are a couple of significant rules when making any yeast product, don't deal with it to an extreme and when to bake it. When you consolidate the ingredients they begin working together and the yeast starts to benefit from the sugars in the flour. This makes carbon dioxide gas which is the thing that makes the bread rise. On the off chance that you can envision a great many tiny bubbles loaded up with gas, the exact opposite thing you need is for those air pockets to burst and be left with a flat, thick bit of dough. That is the reason it's so critical to deal with the dough gently from the moment it begins rising to when it goes in the oven to bake.

HOW DO YOU KNOW WHEN IT'S READY TO BAKE?

Bread and yeast items ordinarily consistently get two times to rise. After the principal rise, you will punch all of the gas out of the dough, however, this is the main time you'll do that. This is to dispose of any huge gas bubbles that may have been made and the yeast will be sufficient for a second rise. It's on this second rise that the bubbles will show up more even and creating a superior texture.

After the second rise is the point at which you'll inevitably move your bread to the oven. The dough should look practically like it would be on the off chance that it was baked. It ought to be genuinely firm and show no air pockets on the external crust. What happens when the dough is left too long to even consider rising and the gas starts to escape from within. This is called"over-proofing". If you somehow managed to bake a loaf this way, it would be flatter and denser because the significant gases got away before you put it in the oven. The key is to keep those gas bubbles intact and inside the dough to end up with a light airy texture.

HANDMADE OLIVE BREAD

Which Yeast Should I Use When I Bake My Olive Bread?

There's dry yeast and new yeast. Dry yeast is the thing that you will find in each supermarket and it comes in minimal square envelopes or little containers. This is by a wide margin the most well-known and simplest approach when preparing bread at home. New yeast arrives in a block and feels like damp clay, and it smells. It's for the most part utilized in bigger commercial pastry shops where they need huge amounts and they can utilize it faster. New yeast should be refrigerated and keeps going just half a month and no more.

Red Star Yeast is my preferred image to utilize with regards to baking bread. They have three distinct kinds of dry yeast to browse contingent upon your recipe plan, and a site loaded up with tips and information sparing me from any catastrophes. I utilized their Platinum yeast which truly accelerated the rising procedure for my olive bread. I've utilized this recipe before with normal yeast and ordinarily needed to let it rise for the time being. Not any longer, I mix this dough at noon and have crackling hot olive bread on the table at dinnertime!

INGREDIENTS

- 3 1/4 cups bread flour in addition to extra for tidying your work surface

- 2 1/2 tsp dynamic dry yeast

- 1 tbsp olive oil to cover the resting bowl

- Cornmeal for tidying

- 1/2 tsp salt

- 1/2 cups warm water

- 1 3/4 cups blended olives pitted and generally cleaved

INSTRUCTIONS

1. Lay a spotless kitchen towel on a cookie plate and dust generously with cornmeal. Put aside with another towel close to it. You will likewise require an enormous dutch stove or overwhelming fired pot with a cover.

2. Combine the flour, yeast, and salt in a stand blender with a dough hook.

3. Add the warm water and delicately mix until the dough comes together.

4. Add the slashed olives and blend until all-around combined.

5. Take the dough out of the bowl and knead delicately into a ball shape.

6. Coat a big bowl with the olive oil and return the dough into its center point.

7. Cover with a spotless towel and Let it sit until it doubles in size.

8. Once it has risen, remove it from the bowl and lay it on your table. Generally, press the dough into a level circle.

9. Fold the dough over on itself kneading it once again into a ball.

10. Lay the dough onto the cornmeal cleaned towel, crease side down.

11. Dust the top of the dough with some additional cornmeal and spread with the towel once more.

12. Let rest until it's nearly multiplied in size once more.

13. Watch it intently and when you see that it's practically prepared, preheat your stove to 450 degrees F and place the vacant pot into it.

14. When the oven has arrived at its temperature, remove the top towel and utilizing a sharp serrated blade, cut two cuts over the top of the dough.

15. Take the pot out of the stove and cautiously lift and drop the bread into the pot.

16. Place the cover on and set it back into the stove. Heat for 30 minutes.

17. After 30 minutes, take the cover from the pot and prepare for a further 20-30 minutes and the outside layer is brilliant and fresh.

18. Let cool before cutting.

Chapter 7:

THE WALNUT COB BREAD RECIPE

Ingredients

- 1 1/2 teaspoons salt

- 6 cups (723g, approx.) Flour

- 1/2 cup (170g) nectar

- 1/4 cup (50g) walnut or olive oil

- 2 cups (227g) walnut pieces, toasted until lightly browned

- 1 1/2 cups (340g) warm water

- 1 tablespoon (11g) dynamic dry yeast

Instructions

1. Dissolve the yeast in the water. Include 1/2 cup (60g) of flour and let sit for 10 minutes to allow the yeast to get moving.

2. Stir in the nectar, oil, and salt.

3. Add the flour, a cup at once, until the dough has shaped

a shaggy mass.

4. Turn the dough out onto a delicately floured counter. Knead the dough, including flour as fundamental, to frame a smooth and silky ball.

5. Put the dough into a bowl and shower with a tablespoon of oil; turn the dough to cover it with the oil.

6. Cover the bowl with plastic wrap or a moist towel. Let the dough rise until it is puffy, around 1/2 hours.

7. Gently empty the dough and work in the walnut.

8. Divide the dough down the middle and structure every half into a ball. Place on a baking sheet that has been fixed with material or lubed and sprinkled with cornmeal or semolina flour.

9. Cover the loaves with moist towels and let rise until swollen. This will take 30-45 minutes.

10. Preheat the oven to 350°F; the loaves will consume if the oven is excessively hot.

11. Sprinkle flour on the top, and utilize a serrated blade to slice a cross in the highest point of each loaf around 1" profound.

12. Bake the loaves for 35-45 minutes, until they are all around brown and sound empty when pounded on the bottom; their inward temperature will gauge 190°F on a moment read thermometer.

13. Put the loaves on a rack to cool, and let sit for in any event 20 minutes before cutting.

Chapter 8:

RYE HOMEMADE BREAD RECIPE

Flavorful Homemade Rye Bread doesn't get a lot less complex than this bakery-style artisan bread. Caraway and rye flour gives the bread its particular flavor. Furthermore, learn to expect the unexpected. No machines required! You can make this bread by hand!

This recipe is excessively easy to assemble, gives some incredible bread-making systems, and makes a dazzling light rye. I've additionally included directions for a dark rye that has cocoa powder and molasses in it if that you'd prefer to take a stab at that.

HOW TO MAKE BAKERY STYLE RYE BREAD:

The way to making incredible bakery-style bread at home is all in the strategy. Bakeries shops use steam stoves to get that great chewy crust. You can make your steam oven by putting a shallow dish of water in the stove with your bread. The water will vanish in the heat, filling your oven with steam.

Utilizing a baking stone or pizza stone is imperative to making both the ideal crust and the ideal crumb. Bread kitchens utilize extravagant ovens of the masonry variety. It's obvious, the oven in your home cooks utilizing transmitted (the fire or the electrical components) and convected heat (the air moving around the oven. A convection stove has fans to aid the course of the air). An oven work stove can utilize conduction on convection and emanated heat. Workmanship oven uses stone, similarly as their name recommends. Stone holds heat truly well. At the point when you put a portion of bread straightforwardly on a hot stone, the stone exchanges its warmth to the bread through conduction. So when you utilize a pizza/preparing stone, you are truly including a third warming technique into your oven.

Ingredients

- 1 1/2 cup rye flour

- 3 cups flour

- 2 tablespoons cornmeal for cleaning

- 1 1/2 tablespoons moment dry yeast

- 2 cups warm water

- 1 1/2 teaspoons salt

- 1 1/2 tablespoons caraway seeds

Cornstarch Wash

- 1/4 cup water

- 1/4 tsp cornstarch

Instructions

1. In the bowl of a stand blender, consolidate the water, yeast, salt, caraway, and rye flour. Include flour 1 cup at once; adding more if important to shape a dough ball that doesn't stick to the sides of the bowl. Dough ought to be delicate, not firm, however, should hold together all alone without being excessively sticky.

2. Transfer to a softly greased huge bowl. Spread with a drying towel and let rise until twofold, around 60 minutes.

3. Shape it into a loaf by extending the dough from the top middle of the dough ball over the edges, and afterward underneath. It should closely resemble you are holding the loaf with two hands and are pulling the dough back to front with your thumbs. Give a few of those pulls with your thumbs until you have a decent looking little loaf.

4. Dust a pizza strip or wooden cutting board with

cornmeal. Put the loaf on the prepared board and let it rise for an additional 40 minutes.

5. Preheat a pizza/preparing stone in the stove to 450 degrees. Place a shallow dish on the rack underneath the baking stone.

6. Dissolve the cornstarch in the 1/4 cup water. Microwave for 45 seconds. Brush the cornstarch fluid on the loaf and cut a few equal lines on the top.

7. Bake the loaf legitimately on the stone. At the point when you put the loaf in, pour a tall glass of water into the shallow skillet underneath. It'll pop and sizzle and steam, so watch your hands. Close the stove entryway and heat for 30 minutes.

Notes

For a dull rye add the accompanying fixings to the mixture:

- 3 tablespoon dull bootstrap molasses

- 1/4 cup unsweetened cocoa powder

Every other fixing and guidelines continue as before.

Chapter 9:

CINNAMON RAISIN WALNUT BREAD RECIPE

A tasty sweet bread formula for you

Fixings:

- 1 large egg (slightly beaten)

- 2 tablespoons shortening, dissolved or at room temperature ((1 ounce))

- ½ cup butter milk or entire milk, at room temperature ((4 ounces))

- ¾ cupwater, at room temperature ((6 ounces))

- 1½ cups raisins washed and drained ((9 ounces))

- 1 cup chopped walnuts ((4 ounces))

- 3½ cups unbleached bread flour ((16 ounces))

- 4 teaspoons granulated sugar

- 1¼ teaspoons salt

- 2 teaspoons instant yeast

- 1¼ teaspoonsground cinnamon

FOR THE TOPPING:

- 2 tablespoons butter (melted)

- ½ cup granulated sugar

- 2 tablespoons ground cinnamon

DIRECTIONS:

1. Stir together the flour, salt, sugar, yeast, and cinnamon in a blending bowl (or in the bowl of an electric blender). Include the egg, buttermilk, shortening, and water. Mix with a huge spoon (or blend on low speed with the paddle attachment) until the ingredients meet up and structure a ball. Alter with flour or water if the dough appears to be excessively sticky or excessively dry and firm.

2. Sprinkle flour on a counter, move the dough to the counter, and start kneading (or blending on medium speed, changing to the dough look). The dough ought to be delicate and flexible, tasteless yet not sticky. Include flour as you knead (or blend), if important, to accomplish this surface. Knead by hand for around 10

minutes (or by machine for 6 to 8 minutes). Sprinkle in the raisins and walnuts during the last 2 minutes of kneading (or blending) to circulate them uniformly and to avoid squashing them to an extreme. (On the off chance that you are blending by machine, you may need to complete the process of kneading by hand to circulate the raisins and walnuts evenly.) The dough should pass through the windowpane test and register 77 to 81 degrees F. Delicately oil a huge bowl and move the dough to the bowl, moving it to cover it with oil. Spread the bowl with plastic wrap.

3. Ferment at room temperature for around 2 hours, or until the dough duplicates in size.

4. Divide the dough into 2 equal pieces and structure them into loaves. Place each loaf in a lightly oiled 8½ by 4½-inch dish, fog the tops with splash oil, and spread freely with plastic wrap.

5. Proof at room temperature for 60 to an hour and a half, or until the dough crests over the lips of the pans and is about multiplied in size.

6. Preheat the oven to 350 degrees F with the oven rack on the center shelf. Place the loaf container on a sheet pan,

ensuring they are not touching one another.

7. Bake the loaves for 20 minutes. Pivot the pan 180 degrees for baking and keep baking for another 20 to 30 minutes, contingent upon the oven. The completed breads should enlist 190 degrees F in the middle and be brilliant brown on top and delicately brilliant on the sides and base. They should make an empty sound when pounded on the bottom.

8. Immediately remove the breads from their pan. Combine the granulated sugar and ground cinnamon for the topping in a shallow plate. Brush the tops of the loaves with softened butter when they come out of the bread pans, and afterward move them in the cinnamon sugar. Cool loaves on a rack for at any rate 60 minutes, ideally 2 hours, before cutting or serving.

Chapter 10:

BRIOCHE BREAD RECIPE

Brioche is viewed as one of the most popular French bread. It is light and sweet yet additionally unimaginably wealthy in flavor which makes it the most versatile breeds. It is delightful with both appetizing foods and sweets.

Brioche dough is very serviceable and not hard to make, however, you might need to spare this recipe for a Saturday morning or a long evening when you have additional opportunity to focus on the calming mood of kneading, molding, chilling, letting rise, and baking required to make the bread. The last advance of eating is an exercise in self-control, as this brioche recipe smells unbelievable as it bakes and you won't have any desire to wait.

When the bread has cooled to sufficiently warm, cut it and present with margarine. Put an extraordinary pot of jam on the table, if you wish, yet it truly isn't required; this brioche is a fantastic independent treat. Brioche is likewise delicious with foie gras.

Ingredients

- 3 tablespoons granulated sugar

- 1 teaspoons salt

- 1 tablespoon moment yeast

- 3 eggs, in addition to 1 egg yolk, beaten together (egg white saved)

- 1/4 cup tepid water

- 10 tablespoons spread

- 2 3/4 cups generally useful flour

- 1/4 cup nonfat dry milk

Steps to Make It

Accumulate the fixings.

1. Using a stand blender fitted with a dough hook, mix the entire ingredient on low speed for 10 minutes, until the dough is smooth and flexible. This procedure can take as long as 15 minutes. On the other hand, you can utilize a bread machine for the kneading part of this recipe. Permit the machine to finish the dough cycle before moving onto the next stage.

2. Gather the dough into a ball and place it in an enormous, greased bowl or mixture holder, going once to cover the

dough. Spread the bowl and afterward permit the dough to ascend for 45 minutes at room temperature; this will launch the maturing procedure to give the brioche its mark enhance. Refrigerate the dough for in any event 8 hours or overnight. Try not to permit the dough to ascend for over 12 hours.

3. Place the risen batter in a greased brioche dish, freely spread it with gently greased plastic wrap, and afterward permit it to rise for an hour and a half to 2 hours until it has multiplied in size. Brush the dough with the saved egg white.

4. Preheat the broiler to 400F. Bake the brioche for 10 minutes. Without opening the oven, reduce the warmth to 350 F, and keep preparing the bread for an extra 30 minutes. The bread is done when an advanced thermometer peruses 190 F. If the bread starts to brown more quickly before it tests done–cover it with foil to abstain from consuming the brioche. Then again, prepare the bread in 12 biscuit tins for 20 to 25 minutes, until they test done.

5. Allow the huge brioche to cool in the search for gold minutes or the individual moves for 5 minutes, and afterward move the bread to a wire rack to cool. For the

best flavor and surface, serve it marginally warm or at room temperature on the primary day. Utilize any day-old brioche in our tasty brioche bread pudding recipe.

Chapter 11:

NO-KNEAD CRUSTY ARTISAN BREAD RECIPE

Artisan bread previously however you've most likely never considered it to be handily made as this! I'd say this is one part recipe, one part magic trick… it's simply mind-boggling. You've got to trust me. The delightful, crusty, and fluffy bread that outcomes from only four ingredients will take your breath away! Everything necessary is flour, yeast, salt, and water, completely turned inside out in a bowl and set to rest for 8-24 hours. Sounds like a lifetime, I know, however holding up is the main troublesome piece of this recipe.

Simply ensure your flour is fresh and yeast isn't expired. I've utilized both dynamic dry yeast and exceptionally dynamic dry yeast with incredible results! Take a look at those scrumptious slices! They're simply asking to be slathered with goat cheddar and nectar, or topped with tomatoes, basil and a shower of good olive oil.

Goodness, the potential outcomes…

I get it, however. You most likely as of now have heaps of inquiries concerning how it's baked, what sort of cookware you can utilize other than a Dutch oven, and to what extent you should let yours rise. The dough just takes 5 minutes to come together, however, it takes some time to rise. All of your understanding thoroughly pays off when this exquisite loaf comes out of your oven, however.

If similar to me, you're remaining there slack-jawed when it's set, you realize you got it right!

I've just made a couple of these marvelous loaves and will make a lot more around the holidays, as well. I can imagine mixing in loads of fun flavorings... rosemary, lemon pizzazz, Parmesan, garlic, and cranberries just to give some examples of thoughts!

1. In a big bowl, mix your flour, yeast, and salt. Make a point to utilize new, non-lapsed ingredients. Pour in warm water and delicately mix until you've made chaotic, shaggy dough. Don't over-work the dough. That is it!

2. Just spread the bowl firmly with plastic wrap and let it settle down anyplace between 8-24 hours at room temperature. You need it to rise and "air pocket" to the surface. I let this dough rise around 9 hours.

3. Once it's risen, place your Dutch oven into a 450 degree F stove to preheat.

4. Meanwhile, pop your dough out onto a very much floured surface. It will be sticky, yet with floured hands, you can without much of a stretch structure it into a round dough ball.

5. Cover it freely with plastic wrap while your Dutch oven preheats. If the cookware you're utilizing isn't enameled or nonstick, slip a bit of material paper underneath the dough now.

6. Carefully remove your Dutch oven from the oven, fly in your dough, and spread it with the top. Once again into the oven, it goes, so set that clock for 30 minutes and trust that the magic will occur!

7. Presently remove the top, set it back in the oven, and bake an extra 7-15 minutes revealed.

8. The revealed baking time just relies upon your broiler. My solitary required 7 additional minutes to get ravishing brilliant brown, yet it can differ. Simply watch out for it.

9. Voila! Pop it out, cut it up, and slather one (or twelve) with butter, STAT.

NO-KNEAD CRUSTY ARTISAN BREAD

YIELD: Makes 1 portion

INGREDIENTS:

- 3 cups universally handy flour

- 2 teaspoons fit salt (not table salt)

- 1/2 teaspoon dry yeast (dynamic dry or exceptionally dynamic dry work best)

- 1/2 cups tepid water

- Extraordinary cookware required: Dutch stove or any huge broiler-safe dish/bowl and lid*

DIRECTIONS:

1. In a big bowl, mix the flour, yeast, and salt. Mix in water utilizing a wooden spoon until the blend frames a shaggy however strong dough. Don't over-work the dough. The less you "work" it, the more delicate, fluffy air pockets will shape.

2. Cover bowl firmly with plastic wrap. Let dough sit at room temperature for 8-24 hours*. Dough will rise and rise.

3. After the dough is prepared, preheat broiler to 450

degrees F. Spot your Dutch oven, revealed, into the preheated oven for 30 minutes.

4. While your Dutch oven preheats, turn dough onto a very much floured surface. With floured hands, structure the dough into a ball. Spread dough freely with plastic wrap and let rest.

5. After the 30 minutes are up, cautiously evacuate Dutch oven. With floured hands, place the bread dough into it. (You can put a bit of material under the dough if your Dutch oven isn't lacquer covered.)

6. Replace cover and prepare for 30 minutes secured. Cautiously remove cover and prepare for 7-15 minutes* increasingly, revealed.

7. Carefully remove bread to a cutting board and cut with a bread blade.

NOTES

Revealed baking time relies upon your oven. In my oven, the bread just needs 7 minutes uncovered until crust up and brilliant brown, however, this can shift. Simply watch out for it!

Preheating your Dutch oven to 450 degrees F won't harm it, or the handle on top.

I've let this dough rise anyplace between 8-24 hours and it has baked up flawlessly. Simply ensure it has risen and seems to "bubble" to the surface.

There's no compelling reason to oil the Dutch oven/baking dish/pot. My bread has never adhered to the pot. If you are concerned, however, put a bit of material paper under your batter before setting into your pot.

I don't prescribe utilizing entire wheat flour or white entire wheat flour in this recipe. The subsequent bread will be thick, and not as cushioned and delightful.

I utilized a 5.5 quart enameled cast iron Le Creuset pot, however, you can utilize any huge stove safe dish and spread. These likewise work: a preparing dish secured with aluminum foil, stewing pot insert, stainless steel pot with a top, pizza stone with an oven-safe bowl to cover the bread, and old cast iron Dutch stove.

Include any blend ins you like - herbs, flavors, dried organic product, cleaved nuts, and cheese all function admirably. I suggest including them into the underlying flour-yeast blend to avoid over-working the mixins into the dough. The less you "work" it, the more you're empowering delicate, fluffy air pockets to frame!

Chapter 12:

CHEESY SEEDED BREADSTICKS RECIPE

Ingredients:

pizza mixture:

- 3 cups bread flour (universally handy is fine)

- 2 1/4 teaspoon moment yeast

- 1 1/2 teaspoons salt

- 2 tablespoons additional virgin olive oil

- 8 ounces warm water

- 1 enormous egg + 1 tablespoons water, beaten

- 2 tablespoons hemp hearts (discretionary)

- 2 ounces ground Parmesan

- 2 tablespoons unsalted margarine, softened and marginally cooled

- 4 ounces destroyed gruyere cheddar (swiss is fine)

- 1/4 cup toasted pumpkin seeds

- 1/4 cup toasted sunflower seeds

Directions:

1. Pizza Dough: Pour flour, salt, yeast, and oil into a combining bowl and whisk. Include water, 1/4 cup water at once, and combine until delicate and sticky mixture structures.

2. Turn dough out onto a clean and daintily floured surface and ply for 2 to 3 minutes, until smooth dough structures.

3. Lightly oil a blending bowl, includes dough and freely spread. Permit dough to rest and twofold in size, around 60 minutes (in a warm, dry spot).

4. Preheat stove to 400°F.

5. Uncover and punch dough in focus. Turn dough out onto a clean and gently floured surface and move until 1/4 inch thick. Trim edges so you have a 16"x 8" square shape.

6. Cut dough into long strips, so there are (16" x 1/2") strips.

7. Generously brush each portion of dough with egg wash

and top with a sprinkle of half the shredded of gruyere. Press down on every breadstick to ensure cheese follows and cautiously bend every breadstick a couple of times and move to a baking sheet fixed with material paper (dividing every breadstick around 1" separated.

8. Lightly brush each stick with dissolved margarine and sprinkle with outstanding gruyere cheese, pumpkin seeds, sunflower seeds, and hemp hearts (if utilizing). Delicately press garnishes into every breadstick and get done with a cleaning of ground Parmesan.

9. Bake breadsticks for 15 to 18 minutes or until brilliant brown.

10. Remove from stove and cool. Serve.

Chapter 13:

PANE PUGLIESE RECIPE

Pane Pugliese is a rural yeasted white bread ordinary of the Puglia area of Italy. In this adaptation, I swap out potato flour for cubes of cooked potato.

Ingredients

For the starter:

- 1/2 cup + 1/2 teaspoons white rye flour

- 1/4 cup + 2 1/2 tablespoons dim rye flour

- generous 1/4 teaspoon moment yeast

- 1/2 cup + 1 teaspoon water at about 60°F (15°C)

For the cooked potatoes: 14 oz unpeeled Yukon gold potatoes, cleaned and cut into 1/4-inch (6 mm) dice

- 2 teaspoons extra-virgin olive oil

- 1/4 teaspoons flaky ocean salt, ideally Maldon

- Dusting Mixture (1 section fine semolina flour and 5 sections white flour), for the lined sealing bin and the formed portion

For the dough:

- 3 cups + 2 1/2 teaspoons white flour, in addition to extra varying for working with the mixture

- 1/2 cup + 1/2 teaspoons medium entire wheat flour

- 2 1/2 teaspoons fine ocean salt

- generous 1/4 teaspoon moment yeast

- 1 1/2 cups + 1 teaspoon water at about 60°F (15°C)

- Dusting Mixture (see above), for the lined sealing container and the formed portion

Headings

Note: The most widely recognized version of Pane Pugliese is a provincial yeasted white bread common of the Puglia area of Italy (which you may have speculated from its name). The adaptation I previously figured out how to make utilized wheat and potato flours and was taught to me by George DePasquale, an Italian-American bread cook in Seattle. I've since built up this form, which joins rye for a full-seasoned starter. Concerning the potato flour, I skipped it and went directly to bits of the entire potato. With no guarantees so regularly the case in bread making, changing this one variable adjusted the character of the bread. The uprightness of leaving the potatoes in little lumps is both surface and flavor. Furthermore, I don't strip the potatoes, since I like the surface of the skin, which dries out during cooking. Along these lines, the potato adds to the last bread similarly olives or raisins do in different breads, giving little islands of flavor and surface in the bigger breadth of scrap. In any case, the potato's commitment truly begins in during the aging stage. The yeast needs to work more diligently and longer to process the potato, and it makes new and differed enhances as it does as such. Be that as it may, unusually, the completed portion doesn't taste firmly of potatoes. I think what happens is that the potato starch transforms into liquor, sugars, and a large number of flavor segments as it separates and joins with different ingredients. Not long before preparing, the completed batter smells sweet and supporting, especially like a wheat brew. One of my ordinary clients consistently purchases a large portion of a loaf at once, clarifying that he's so dependent on this bread if he purchased the entire loaf, he would return for another similarly as regularly, so he'd eat twice as much bread in a similar measure of time. My inquiry is, What's the issue with that?

1. For the starter: Stir together the white and dim rye flours in a medium stockpiling container. Sprinkle the yeast into the water, mix to blend, and pour over the flour.

Blend in with your fingers, squeezing the mixture into the sides, base, and corners until the entirety of the flour is wet and completely joined. Spread the container and let sit at room temperature for 11 to 15 hours. The starter will be at its top at around 13 hours.

2. For the simmered potatoes: Preheat the stove to 400°F (205°C). Put the potatoes in a bowl. Greased with the oil and sprinkle with the salt, at that point toss until equitably covered. Spread on a half sheet pan and bake until the skin is brilliant brown and the potatoes are delicate around 25 minutes. The potatoes will decrease in weight when roasted. You will require 200 grams (1/2 cups) of roasted potatoes for this recipe. Let cool totally, at that point refrigerate until prepared to utilize.

3. For the dough: Stir together the white and entire wheat flours, salt, and yeast in a medium bowl.

4. Pour around 33% of the water around the edges of the starter to discharge it from the sides of the holder. Move the starter and water to an extra-\large bowl alongside the rest of the water. Utilizing a wooden spoon, split the starter up to appropriate it in the water.

5. Add the flour mixture, saving around one-6th of it along

the edge of the bowl. Keep on mixing in with the spoon until the greater part of the dry ingredients have been joined with the starter mix. Change to a plastic bowl scrubber and keep on mixing until joined. Now the dough will be sticky to the touch.

6. Push the mixture to the other side of the bowl. Roll and fold the dough, including the held flour mixture and a modest quantity of extra flour to the bowl and your hands varying. Keep rolling and tucking until the mixture feels more grounded and starts to oppose any further moving, around multiple times. At that point, with measured hands, fold the sides under toward the middle. Spot the mixture, fold side down, in a perfect bowl, spread the top of the bowl with a spotless kitchen towel, and let rest at room temperature for 45 minutes.

7. For the main stretch and overlap, softly dust the work surface and your hands with flour. Utilizing the plastic bowl scrubber, discharge the dough from the bowl and set it, fold side down, on the work surface. Delicately stretch it into a rectangular shape. Fold the dough in thirds through and through and afterward from left to right. With measured hands, fold the sides under toward the inside. Spot the dough in the bowl, fold side down,

spread the bowl with the towel, and let rest for 45 minutes.

8. For the subsequent stretch and fold, repeat the means for the main stretch and overlap, at that point return the mixture to the bowl, spread with the towel, and let rest for 45 minutes.

9. For the third and last stretch and fold, tenderly stretch the dough into a square shape, disperse the potatoes over the top, and delicately press them into the mixture. Move up the dough firmly from the end nearest to you; toward the finish of the roll, the mixture will be fold side down. Turn it over, fold side up, and tenderly push on the fold to level the dough somewhat. Fold in thirds from left to right and afterward do one roll and fold succession to join the potatoes. Turn the dough, fold side down and fold the sides under toward the middle. Return the fold to the bowl, spread with the towel, and let rest for 20 minutes.

10. Line a 9-inch (23-centimeter) sealing bushel or bowl with a perfect kitchen towel and residue the towel reasonably liberally with the cleaning mixture.

11. Lightly residue the work surface and your hands with

flour, and shape the dough into a round. Residue the sides and top of the dough with the cleaning mixture, fold the edges of the towel over the top, and let rest at room temperature for 60 minutes.

12. Transfer the crate to the fridge and chill for 14 to 18 hours.

13. Position a stove rack in the lower third of the oven. Place a secured 6-quart (5.7-liter), 10-inch (25-centimeter) round cast-iron Dutch oven on the rack. Preheat the oven to 500°F (260°C).

14. Remove the crate of mixture from the cooler and let it sit at room temperature while you permit the oven to preheat for around 60 minutes.

15. Using hardcore stove gloves or potholders, evacuate the Dutch oven, place it on a heatproof surface, and remove the cover.

16. Using the kitchen towel, lift and tenderly facilitate the dough out of the container and onto a preparing strip, fold side down. At that point cautiously move it into the pot (the Dutch oven will be hot). Score the highest point of the dough, spread the pot, and return it to the stove. Lower the oven temperature to 460°F (240°C) and

prepare for 30 minutes.

17. Rotate the Dutch oven and remove the top. The portion will as of now be a rich brilliant brown colored. Keep baking, uncovered, until the surface is a deep, rich brown, with certain places along the score being even somewhat darker (bien cuit), around 20 minutes longer.

18. Loosen the edges of the loaf with a since quite a while ago dealt with spoon and afterward with the assistance of the spoon lift out of the pot onto a cooling rack. At the point when the base of the portion is tapped, it should sound empty. If not, return it to the oven and prepare legitimately on the rack for 5 minutes longer.

19. Let the bread cool totally before cutting and eating, in any event, 4 hours yet ideally 8 to 24 hours.

Chapter 14:

NATURAL BROWN BREAD RECIPE

Ingredients

- 400g malted grain earthy colored bread flour, or wholemeal or storage facility bread flour

- 100g solid white bread flour

- 7g sachet simple heat dried yeast (or 2 tsp Quick dried yeast)

- 1½ tsp salt

- 1 tbsp delicate margarine

- 4 tbsp blended seed (discretionary, for example, linseed, pumpkin, sesame, and sunflower, in addition to extra for sprinkling

Method

Mix your choice of brown flour in with the white, the yeast, and salt in a huge mixing bowl. Put in the margarine and rub it into the flour. Mix in the seeds if utilizing. Make a plunge in the center of the flour and pour in practically 300ml hand warm (cool as opposed to high temp) water, with a round-bladed blade.

At that point mix in enough of the rest of the water and more if necessary, to get together any dry bits in the base of the bowl and until the mixture comes together as a delicate, not very sticky, mixture. Accumulate it into a ball with your hands.

Put the dough on to a daintily floured surface and work for 8-10 mins until it feels smooth and versatile, possibly including the base of additional flour if important to forestall the mixture staying. Spot the wad of mixture on a gently floured work surface. Spread with an improved, perfect, enormous glass bowl and leave for 45 mins-1 hr or until multiplied in size and feels light and springy. Timing will rely upon the glow of the room.

Thump back the mixture by softly plying only 3-4 times. You just need to take out any huge air bubbles, so an excess of taking care of now will lose the mixture's softness. Shape into a ball. Spread with the glass bowl and leave for 15 mins.

Presently shape to make a tin portion Grease a 1.2-liter limit portion tin (around 23 x 13 x 5.5cm) and line the base with preparing material. Utilizing your knuckles, straighten the mixture into a square shape around 25 x 19cm. Fold both shorter closures into the inside like an envelope, make a ¼ turn, at that point straighten again into a similar size and move up firmly, beginning from one of the short finishes. Roll the top of the dough in additional seeds and spot in the tin with the join underneath, squeezing the seeds tenderly into the dough. Spread with a spotless tea towel. Leave for 40-45 mins, or until rise about 5cm over the top of the tin.

Put a cooking tin in the base of the oven 20 mins before prepared to prepare and warm stove to 230C/210C fan/gas 8. Put the risen bread in the oven, cautiously empty about 250ml virus water into the cooking tin (this will murmur and make an eruption of steam to give you a fresh outside), at that point bring down the warmth to 220C/200C fan/gas 7. Bake for around 30 mins or until brilliant, covering with foil for the last 5 mins if beginning to brown too rapidly. Leave in the tin for 2-3 mins, at that point evacuate and cool on a wire rack. On the off chance that you tap the underneath of the baked loaf if ought to be firm and sound empty.

Chapter 15:

BANANA BREAD RECIPE

1 (8-inch) portion, handily duplicated

INGREDIENTS

- Cooking shower

- 8 tablespoons (1 stick) unsalted margarine

- 1 cup granulated sugar

- 2 enormous eggs

- 1/4 cup milk

- 1 teaspoon vanilla concentrate

- 3 medium bananas, extremely ready

- 2 cups universally handy flour

- 1 teaspoon heating pop

- 1/4 teaspoon salt

- 1/2 cup slashed nuts or chocolate chips (discretionary)

EQUIPMENT

- 1 8x5-inch portion container

- Parchment paper

- Large bowl

- Whisk or fork, if making by hand

- Stand blender or hand blender, if not made by hand

- Spatula

Directions

1. Heat the oven to 350°F and prepare the container. Organize a rack in the base third of the oven and warmth to 350°F. Line an 8x5-inch loaf pan with material paper, letting the overabundance hang over the long sides to shape a sling. Shower within with cooking splash. → If utilizing nuts, toast them in the oven for 10 minutes as the oven is pre-warming.

2. Melt the spread. Dissolve the margarine in the microwave or over low warmth on the stovetop. → Alternatively, for a more cake-like banana bread, mollify the spread (however don't soften) and cream it with the sugar in a stand blender in the following stage.

3. Mix the margarine and sugar. Spot the liquefied margarine and sugar in a big bowl and whisk until consolidated. (Or then again cream the mollified spread and sugar in a blender until fluffy.)

4. Add the eggs. Break the eggs into the bowl. Whisk until joined and the mix is smooth.

5. Add the milk and vanilla. Whisk the milk and vanilla into the player.

6. Mash in the bananas. Strip the bananas and add them to the bowl. Utilizing the finish of the whisk or a supper fork, pound them into the player. Leave the bananas as stout or as smooth as you usually like. If you favor a smooth banana bread, crush the bananas independently until no more lumps remain, and afterward whisk them into the batter.

7. Add the flour, heating pop, and salt. Measure the flour, preparing pop, and salt into the bowl. Change to utilizing a spatula and tenderly mix until the fixings are scarcely joined and not any more dry flour is obvious.

8. Fold in the nuts or chocolate, if utilizing. To wrap things up, dissipate the nuts or chocolate over the batter and delicately crease them in.

9. Pour the batter into the container. Empty the batter into the readied loaf container, utilizing the spatula to scratch all the batter from the bowl. Smooth the highest point of the batter.

10. Bake for 50 to 65 minutes. Prepare until the top of the cake is caramelized dull brown with some yellow inside looking through and a toothpick or cake analyzer embedded into the center confesses all, 50 to 65 minutes. Heating time will fluctuate marginally relying upon the dampness and sugar substance of your bananas — begin checking around 50 minutes and afterward at regular intervals after.

11. Cool in the search for gold minutes. Set the loa, still in the container, on a wire cooling rack. Let it cool for 10 minutes — this enables the portion to harden and makes it simpler to remove from the container.

12. Remove from the container and cook an additional 10 minutes. Getting a handle on the material paper sling, lift the portion out of the container and spot on the cooling rack. Cool for an additional 10 minutes before cutting.

Chapter 16:

HOMEMADE CORNBREAD RECIPE

This cornbread has been a staple for my family for a considerable length of time and years, however, I understood some time back that I hadn't made a post to impart it to you! My family completely adores this cornbread and I'm certain your friends and family will as well.

This cornbread is EASY. No buttermilk. Prepare it in any pan. Prepared in a short time!

One reason I love this cornbread recipe is that you needn't bother with anything extravagant to make it. Many cornbread recipes require buttermilk or creamed corn or a quite certain sort of dish. By correlation, my recipe is one you can make quickly, whenever, with what you have close by. You can utilize any sort of pan and needn't bother with any unique ingredients. With only a couple of things, you most likely as of now have close by you can make the best cornbread ever!

What makes this the Best Cornbread?

Well first off, it tastes DIVINE. It's sweet however not over the top, delicate yet not cakey, and brittle without being a plane wreckage. I can't suggest it enough!

Cornbread Ingredients:

1. All reason flour: All reason flour will permit the bread to rise a piece and give it the light, cake consistency of bread.

2. Yellow cornmeal: An unquestionable requirement for cornbread! It gives the bread its delightful brilliant brown shading and the grainy, scrumptious consistency.

3. Granulated sugar: This gives the bread a pinch of sweetness it needs to adjust the corn and bread flavors.

4. Salt: Just a squeeze to draw out the multifaceted nature of flavors.

5. Baking powder: To enable the batter to rise and grow as it prepares.

6. Butter: This is an absolute necessity — it gives the bread a soggy, flaky, rich flavor that is magnificent.

7. Egg: This ties everything together and causes the bread to rise.

8. Milk: For a rich, damp cornbread!

The most effective method to Make Cornbread

Alright, presently how about we get to the subject of this post: how to make hand made cornbread! You might be amazed to find that heating an ideal pan of cornbread just requires a couple of simple advances:

1. Grease a 9-inch round cake dish or throw iron pan well and set away. Preheat the oven to 400 degrees F.

2. In a medium blending bowl, include the cornmeal, sugar, salt, flour, and preparing powder. Speed to consolidate well.

3. Make a well in the center of your dry ingredients and include your oil or spread, milk, and egg. Mix just until the dough comes together and there is just a couple of bumps remaining.

4. Pour the batter into the readied container and bake for 20-25 minutes until the top is a deep brilliant brown and a toothpick embedded into the middle confesses all.

5. Serve hot.

Chapter 17:

PORTUGUESE SWEET BREAD RECIPE

This delicate, ameliorating bread is a backbone among Portuguese bread sweethearts, particularly at Christmas (and Easter, when it encases a bubbled egg). In this nation, the round, mahogany-shaded portion regularly incorporates inconspicuous traces of both lemon and vanilla. While it's generally served plain or with margarine, it additionally makes delectable toast (or French toast). Our variant of this bread isn't as sweet nor rich as a few; we found that a high proportion of sugar, eggs, and margarine to flour hinders the yeast so much that the portion doesn't rise well. In any case, we're certain you'll appreciate this somewhat sweet bread nonetheless.

Ingredients

- 1/2 cup (113g) milk

- 1/4 cup (4 tablespoons, 57g) margarine, cut into taps

- 1/3 cup (67g) sugar

- 1 1/4 teaspoons salt

- 3 1/4 cups (390g) King Arthur Unbleached All-Purpose Flour

- 1 tablespoon moment yeast, SAF Gold moment yeast favored ground strip (get-up-and-go) of 1 medium lemon

- 2 enormous eggs + 1 huge egg yolk, white held

- 2 teaspoons vanilla concentrate

Guidelines

1. Combine the margarine, sugar, milk, and salt in a microwave-safe cup or a pot. Warmth to tepid, mixing to relax the margarine. Put in a safe spot.

2. In a mixing bowl, the bowl of your stand blender, or the basin of your bread machine, consolidate the flour, yeast, and lemon pizzazz; mix to join.

3. Add the milk blend, mixing first to ensure the sugar and salt aren't left in the base of the cup or dish.

4. Add the eggs, yolk, and vanilla. Blend and ply until the batter is strong and smooth; it'll be sticky from the start. In case you're utilizing a stand blender, beat with the level mixer for around 3 minutes at medium-fast; at that point scratch the mixture into the center of the bowl, change to the batter snare, and massage for around 5

minutes at medium speed. It will have shaped a ball fairly, however, will presumably still be adhering to the base of the bowl. In case you're utilizing a bread machine let it experience its whole cycle, and jump to stage 6.

5. Lightly oil the blending bowl or a huge (8-cup) measure, round the batter into a ball, and spot it in the bowl or measure. Spread, and let rise until puffy, around 1/2 to 2 hours. In case you're utilizing a bread machine and the batter hasn't multiplied in size when the cycle is finished, essentially let it rest in the machine for another 30 to an hour.

6. Lightly oil a 9" round cake pan, or a preparing sheet. The round container will make a to some degree taller portion.

7. Gently collapse the mixture, and round it into a ball. Spot the ball in the container or on the preparing sheet, and tent the batter tenderly with delicately lubed plastic wrap. Or then again spread it with your preferred front.

8. Let the loaf rise for around 2 hours, until it's pleasantly puffy. Around the finish of the rising time, preheat the oven to 350°F.

9. Mix the saved egg white with 1 tablespoon cold water, and brush some onto the outside of the loaf; this will give it a silky, mahogany-brown hull.

10. Bake the bread for 15 minutes, at that point tent it delicately with aluminum foil. Bake for an extra 20 to 25 minutes, until it's a medium brilliant brown and its inside temperature registers 190°F on a computerized thermometer.

11. Remove the bread from the oven, and tenderly exchange it to a rack to cool. Cool totally before cutting.

12. Store for a few days at room temperature all around wrapped; freeze for longer stockpiling.

Chapter 18:

PANETTONE [ITALIAN CHRISTMAS BREAD] RECIPE

This formula makes a delightful, delicate, supple mixture that is a lot of like a brioche. Added to the mixture is half of a vanilla bean (which is expelled before heating), rum-splashed raisins, and sugar-coated orange strip. This bread is a genuine work of art. It's staggering, and the flavor satisfies its looks. The bread is fantastically delicate and sweet and simply stacked with season on account of the vanilla bean, lemon get-up-and-go, raisins, and sugar-coated orange strip.

A formula for Panettone, Italian Christmas bread, with a brioche-like batter injected with a vanilla bean and studded with rum-drenched raisins and sugar-coated orange strip.

Ingredients

- 1 cupraisins

- 2 tablespoons light rum

- 2 tablespoons hot water

- 3¾ cupsall-reason flour

- ⅔ cup granulated sugar

- ⅔ cup tepid water

- 1 tablespoon honey

- 10 ½ tablespoons unsalted butter (well mellowed)

- 1 tablespoon unsalted butter (melted)

- 1 tablespoon unsalted butter (chilled)

- ⅔ cup candied citron (I utilized sugar coated orange strip in ¼-inch pieces)

- ½ teaspoon active dry yeast

- ½ teaspoon salt

- ¼ teaspoon lemon pizzazz

- ½ vanilla bean (split into equal parts the long way)

- 3 eggs (at room temperature)

Unique EQUIPMENT: Panettone molds

- (6x4½-inch - Flour)

- 12-inch metal or wooden sticks

Bearings:

1. In a little bowl, consolidate the raisins with the rum and 2 tablespoons of heated water. Permit to splash at room temperature, mixing every so often, until the raisins are stout and a large loaf of the fluid has been retained, in any event, 8 hours or overnight.

2. In a stand blender fitted with an oar connection, combine the flour, yeast, salt, sugar, lemon pizzazz, and vanilla bean on low speed until consolidated. In a medium bowl, whisk together the eggs, lukewarm water, and nectar. With the blender on low speed, empty the egg blend into the flour blend. Speed up to medium-low and blend until the entirety of the ingredients are consolidated. Include the mellowed margarine, 1 tablespoon at once, mixing until consolidated before including more. Speed up to medium-high and beat until the batter is smooth and flexible around 8 minutes.

3. Drain the raisins, dispose of the dousing fluid, and mix with the sweetened citron and 1 tablespoon of softened spread. Mix this blend into the mixture with a wooden spoon.

4. Place the mixture in a big bowl, spread with plastic

wrap, and let rise in a cool broiler with the entryway shut until it has almost significantly increased in volume, 12 to 15 hours.

5. Locate and remove the vanilla bean, at that point sprinkle the mixture gently with flour and scratch out onto a softly floured surface. Sprinkle more flour onto the batter, at that point overlap the edges of the mixture in towards the inside, framing a free ball, and spot, crease side down, into the panettone shape. Spread with a soggy kitchen towel (not terry fabric) and let rise in a without draft place at warm room temperature until the batter is simply over the top of the form, 3 to 5 hours.

6. Preheat stove to 370 degrees F.

7. Place the batter filled panettone form on a heating sheet. Utilize a sharp serrated blade to score an "X" over the whole surface of the batter. Spot the 1 tablespoon chilled spread in the center point of the X and bake until a wooden stick embedded into the middle comes out marginally damp yet not wet, 60 to 75 minutes (the panettone will be dull).

8. Remove from the oven and penetrate 12-inch metal or wooden sticks right through the panettone (counting the

paper) 4 inches separated and 1 inch from the base so the sticks are equal. Hang the panettone topsy turvy over an enormous stockpot and cool totally before cutting. To store the panettone, wrap firmly in saran wrap, at that point either place in a resealable plastic pack, or wrap again in foil. The bread will keep at room temperature for as long as multi-week. (I have not taken a stab at freezing the bread, however, I trust it would freeze well, enclosed by plastic, at that point foil, at that point put in a resealable sack.)

Chapter 19:

CONCLUSION

The way to accomplishing wonderful Artisan bread is to look at one of the most misjudged equipment in the bread baking process - the oven.

Ovens that are utilized broadly for quite a long time will, in general, give off base readings of the temperature. Now and again the warmth you point the switch on isn't what's impacting inside. To know whether your oven is as yet working at its best, use oven thermometers. These are handily obtained in café supply shops. You can even locate these on the web. There are easy way for knowing whether your oven is still ready for action how it should. That is utilizing your understanding and involvement with utilizing a similar oven for quite a long time.

Observe and recollect the temperatures you use when you bake various types of food, going from meat, cakes, to your Artisan bread. Knowing the result and the procedure you utilized in baking will show you the status of your oven. So if there are any unexpected differences in the result, provided that you are consistent with the ingredients and preparation, you will get an idea that something must not be wrong with your oven.

It is a given that the oven is significant in all parts of baking.

So it is on the whole correct to state that an oven with an exact temperature is an absolute necessity. In those days, Artisan bakers truly utilize a hearth made of stone to accomplish ideal warmth because a hot oven is the way into an astonishing crumb and crust.

Since it isn't practical to have your hearth uniquely made, ensuring that your oven is as hot as it was the point at which it was fresh out of the box new will render you the great Artisan breads you want. That is because an extremely hot oven springs up the dough the second it is placed in because of how it gets loaded up with sight-seeing and direct warmth. The oven assumes a significant job in preparing not just because it's chiefly utilized as the last advance in the baking procedure, yet also since it is the place a major white mass of dough turns into an extraordinary crusty up Artisan bread.

Made in the USA
Monee, IL
25 May 2020